Encounter:

A Collection of Inspired Art

Carolyn Charismata Weaver

Published in the United States by BH Publishing
First BH Press Edition, 2023

ISBN: 978-1-7349297-5-1

Dedication

This book is dedicated to the door, the gateway to the heavenlies, who is also my best friend, Jesus! I'm so grateful that He holds all of time in His hands, and He is always at work in us to bring about a good plan for our lives.

It is also dedicated to my husband, Paul, who always stands by me and supports my dreams, sometimes more than I believe in them. Thank you, sweetheart, for being so amazing!

Introduction

This book is a collection of acrylic paintings which utilize pour techniques along with painting images seen within the designs. As I began to see in my mind's eye these images emerging, a new, artistic adventure was birthed for me. Many intercessors and artist have repetitively visualized similar themes for the past couple of decades. I believe that's because these are themes on the heart of God.

Each piece of artwork represents a message for the current times as inspired by the Holy Spirit. God is the ultimate creator. We are made in His image to be creative. As we partner with God through the creative process, we release His will through what we create here on earth.

"Our Father, who is in heaven... your kingdom come, and your will be done on earth as it is in heaven." Matt. 6: 9-10 AMP

It is time for the artisans to connect with heaven to portray the heart of God for this season, as conduits for heaven to be released here on earth. As we connect with God in heavenly places, where we are already seated with Him, we can then release the message that He gives us on earth. We are creative warriors, bringing heaven to earth for His glory and honor.

I pray you will encounter the heart of God as you explore this collection of art.

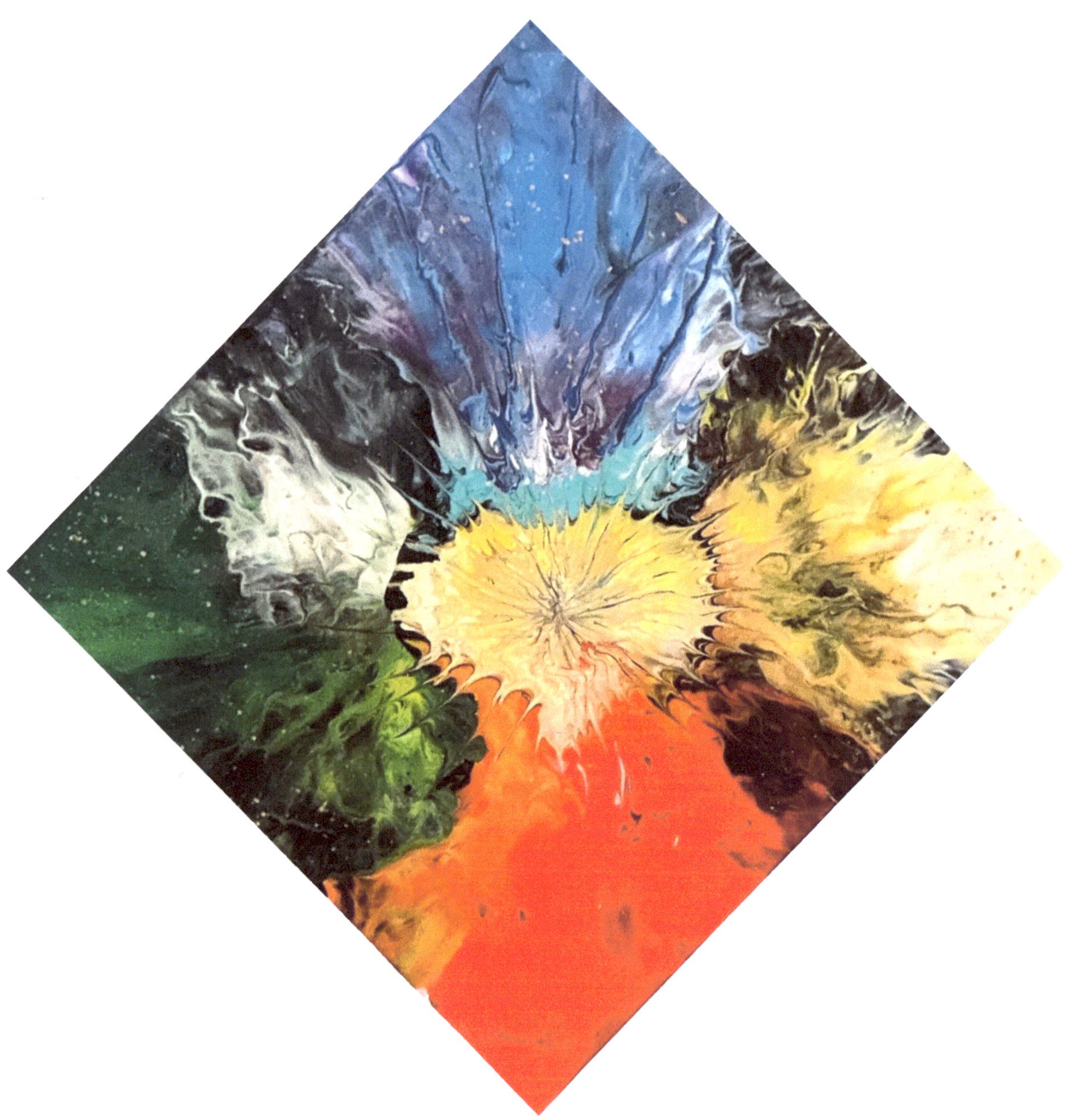

Carolyn Weaver, *The Fifth Element*, 2022, Acrylics, 18" x 18", Simpsonville, SC, USA @Carolyn Weaver.

The Fifth Element

"For even the whole creation, all of nature, waits eagerly for the children of God to be revealed...." Romans 8:19 AMP

As I began to look at the elements of creation and colors to represent them, I decided to try a pour where the colors are blown out from the middle. Then, I felt led to put white, yellow, and gold in the middle, to represent the Holy Spirit's life-giving breath in all of creation.

When the painting dried, I realized that the colors in the middle formed a heart. It is God's breath of love, the fifth element, intertwined in all the other elements of creation that brings life to earth.

All of creation is groaning for the revelation of the Sons and Daughters of God, and as we are revealed "creation itself will also be freed from its bondage to decay into the glorious freedom of the children of God." Romans 8:21 Amp

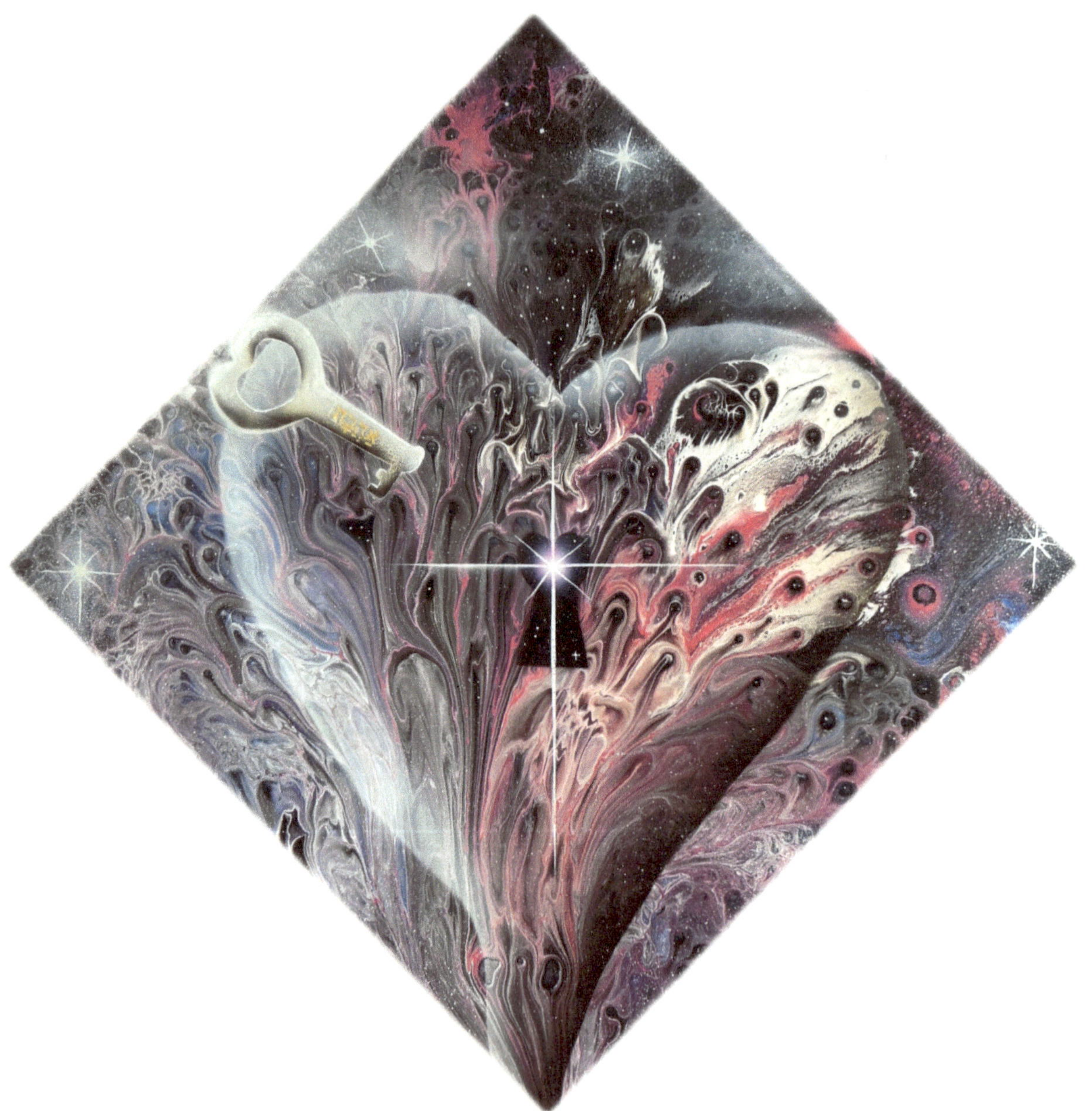

Carolyn Weaver, *The Key to God's Heart*, 2021, Acrylics, 20" x 20",

Simpsonville, SC, USA @Carolyn Weaver.

The Key to God's Heart

"I am convinced that nothing can ever separate us from God's love." Romans 8:38 NLT

I've always thought that God's love was the key to open our heart, and it is, but as I saw this painting in my mind's eye, Yahweh said, "My children are the KEY to My heart, and that key is LOVE." God opens His heart to us as we chose to respond in LOVE to Him.

All Love originates in His heart, and His love casts out all FEAR. As we receive His unconditional, endless, passionate love, we unlock even more by our response of love given back to Him. We hold the Key to God's heart of LOVE!

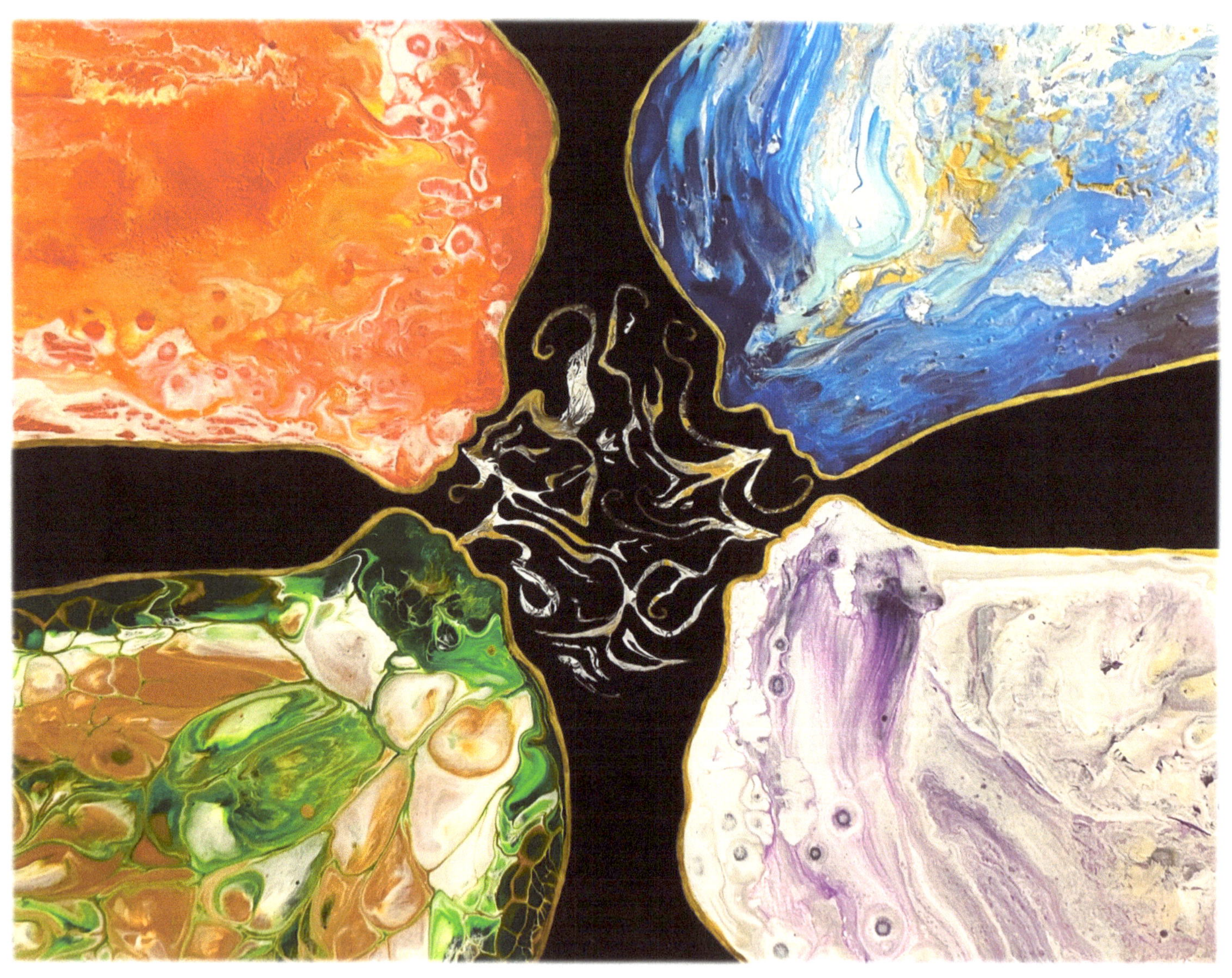

Carolyn Weaver, *The Four Winds*, 20221, Acrylics, 20" x 16",

Simpsonville, SC, USA @Carolyn Weaver.

The Four Winds

"After this, I saw four angels standing at the four corners of the earth, restraining the four winds of the earth..." Rev. 7:1 CSB

"...Breathe, come from the four winds and breathe into these slain so that they may live!" Ezekiel 37:9 CSB

In this painting, I explored the idea of the four archangels interacting with the four elements of earth, while standing at the four corners of the earth. With the power of the Holy Spirit's breath, they restore, create, resurrect the dry bones that have long since died, so that they will live again!"

Yahweh is raising up an end time army, resurrecting the dry, dead bones in our lives to create the new man, a new creation filled with the Spirit of God!

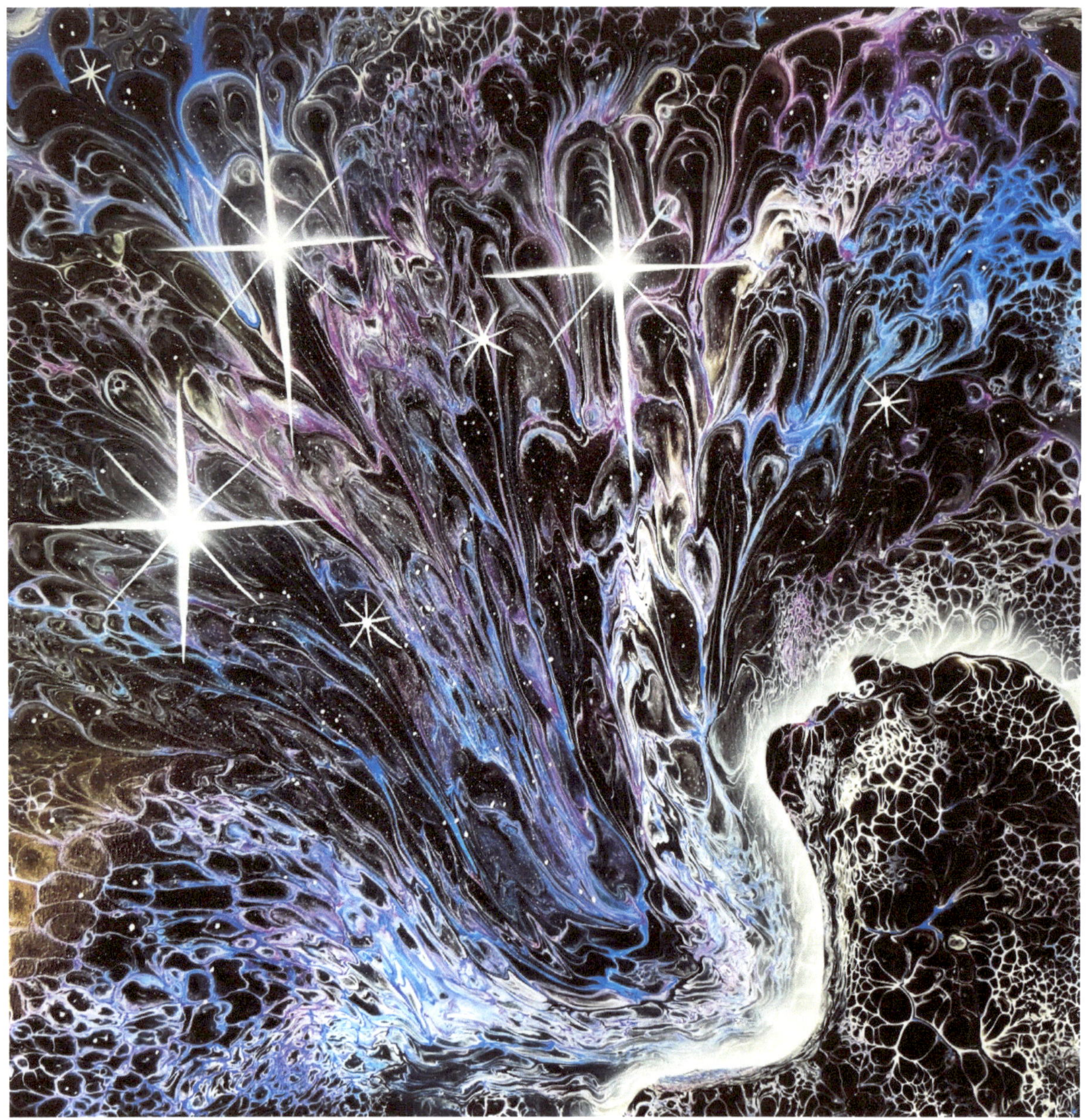

Carolyn Weaver, *The Encounter,* 2022, Acrylics, 20" x 20",

Simpsonville, SC, USA @Carolyn Weaver.

The Encounter

"Yes, feast on all the treasures of the heavenly realm and fill your thoughts with heavenly realities, and not with the distractions of the natural realm." Colossians 3:2 TPT

This painting is an expression of what it may look like for mankind to be connected to the heavenly realm through Jesus.

As this painting dried after I had poured it, there was a natural line created where the face appeared. I simply highlighted it. It felt like a holy kiss of heaven, in which God was saying that He longs for us to connect with Him, even far more than we want to connect with Him.

God desires for us to connect with the heavenly realm with and through Jesus, so that He flows into us and through us to change the environments around us.

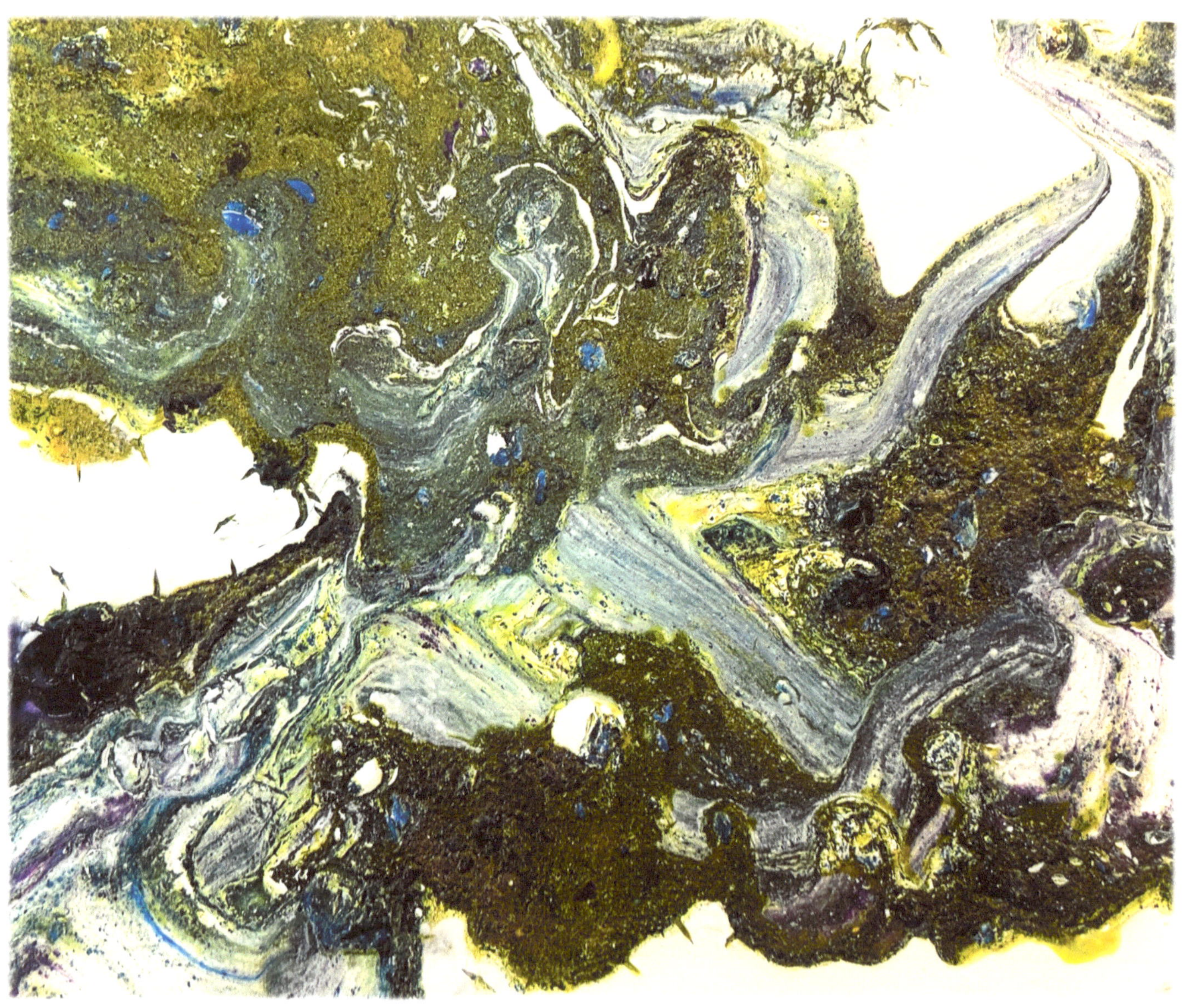

Carolyn Weaver, *Eden Arising*, 2022, Acrylics, 11" x 14",

Simpsonville, SC, USA @Carolyn Weaver.

Eden Arising

"Behold, I am creating new heavens and a new earth; And the former things of life will not be remembered or come to mind." Isaiah 65:17 AMP

This painting was a bit of an accident, but quickly became one of my favorite pieces, because it represented something I've seen in the Spirit for a while.

As we get closer to the end of this age and the dawning of the next one, it feels like the old earth and the new heavenly kingdom are on a collision course. As the old Eden arises to meet the new Kingdom Realm, the birthing of the next age bursts forth.

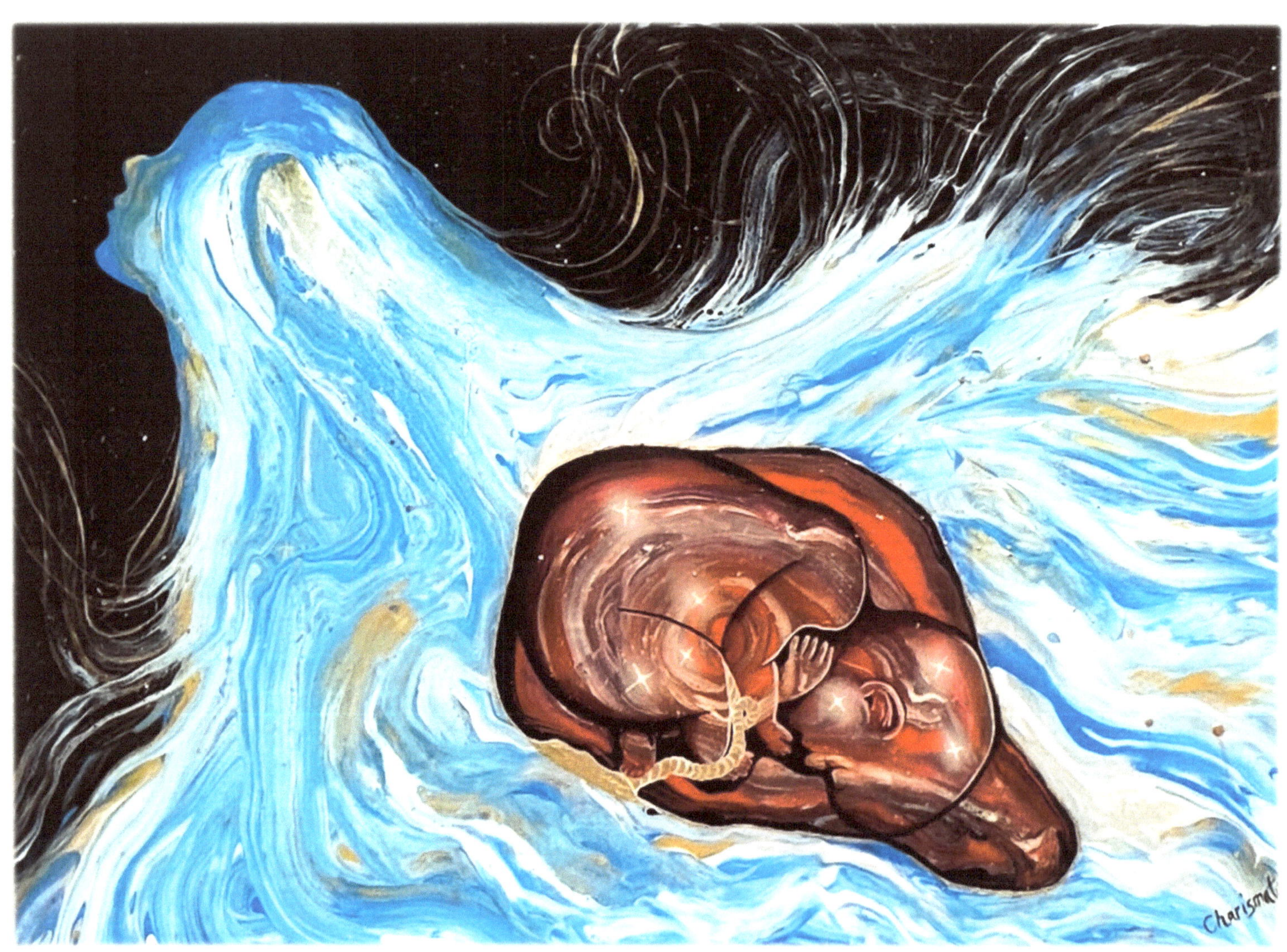

Carolyn Weaver, *The Birthing*, 2021, Acrylics, 27" x 38",
Simpsonville, SC, USA @Carolyn Weaver.

The Birthing

"Then I saw a new heaven and a new earth; for the first heaven and the first earth had passed away (vanished)..."
Revelation 21:1 AMP

As I was spending time with Jesus, I felt an invitation from Him to come. He took me by the hand, and suddenly, we weren't on earth anymore, but in the heavens, surrounded by stars and planets.

Before me, the Holy Spirit flowed fluidly like a great ocean wave - a great outpouring.

Inside the Holy Spirit, in the womb of God, was a baby with galaxies inside of him. The Spirit is about to give birth to this new child. The next chapter in the grand story is about to push through.

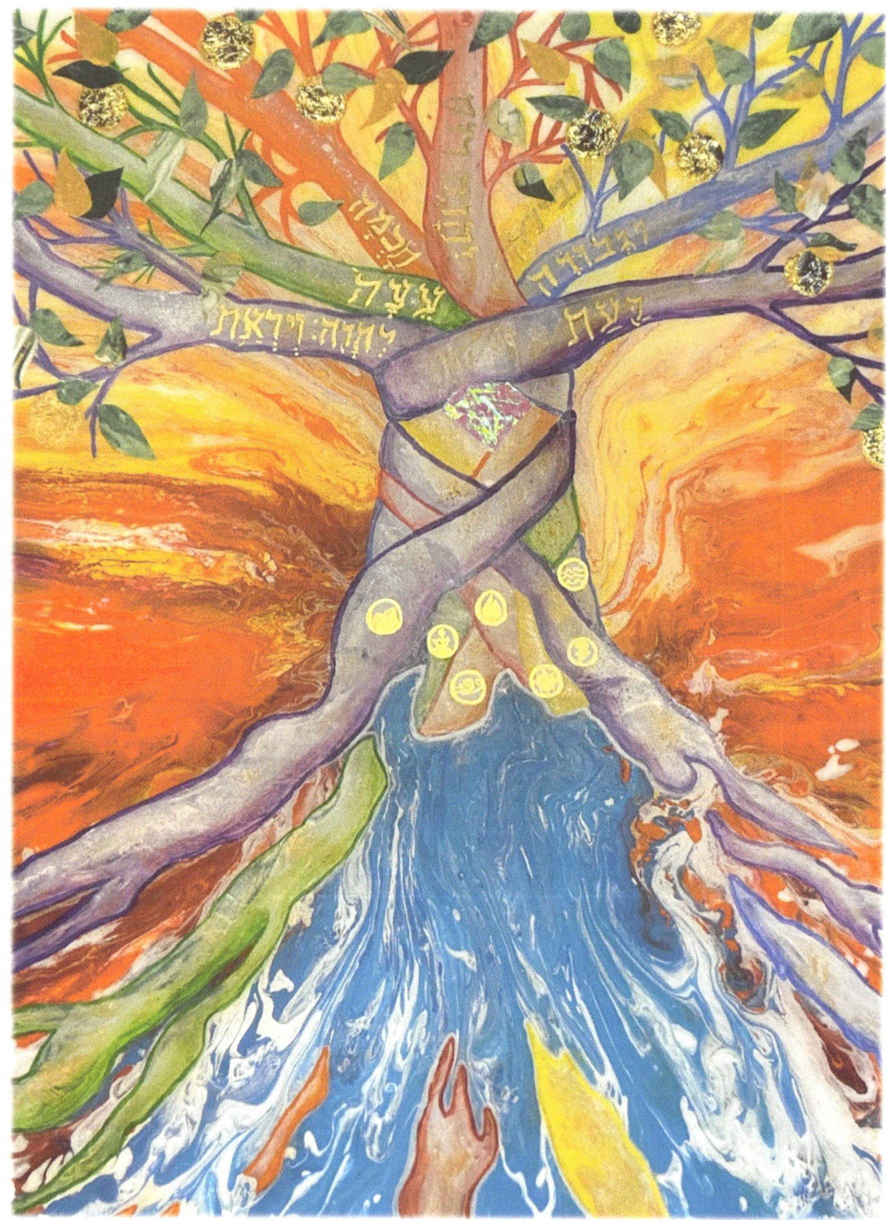

Carolyn Weaver, *The Tree of Life,* 2022, Acrylics, 27" x 38",

Simpsonville, SC, USA @Carolyn Weaver.

The Tree of Life

"On either side of the river was the tree of life, bearing twelve kinds of fruit, yielding it's fruit every month; and the leaves of the tree were for the healing of the nations."
Revelations 22:2 AMP

This painting began with a vision. As I stepped into the tree of life, I was surrounded by pulsating, swirling ribbons of colors that encased me inside, feeding me with nourishing light and energy.

As I attempted to paint what I had experienced, a diamond in the center formed through the ribbons, and I realized that we are the connection through the power of the Spirit for the Seven Spirits of the God (Isaiah 11:2) to flow through to redeem the seven aspects of earth as found in St. Patrick's prayer (see reference at the end).

The river of life from the Holy Spirit also flows through us, and the tree of Life bears good fruit in us, which brings healing to the nations.

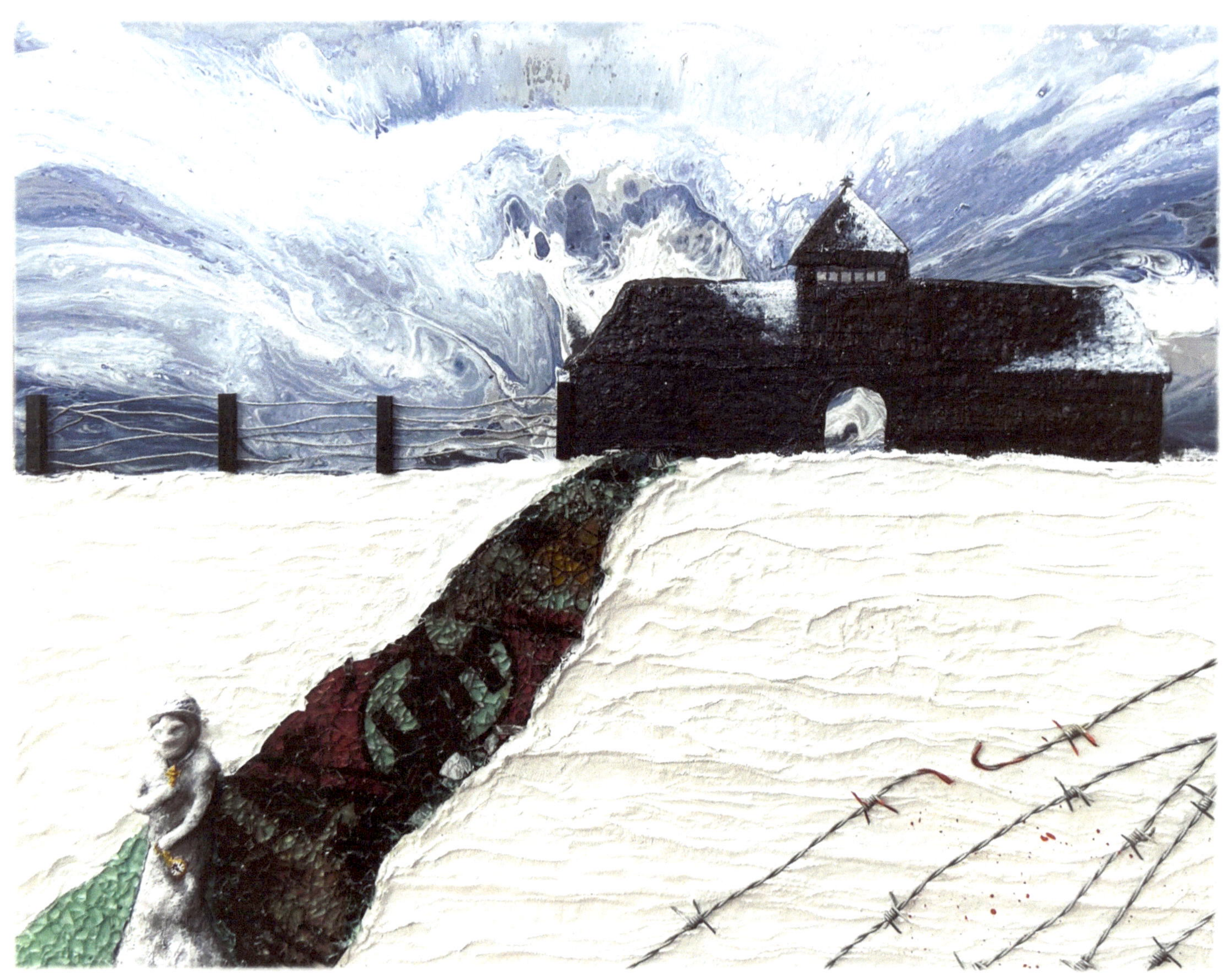

Carolyn Weaver, *It's Time*, 2022, Acrylics, 22" x 28",

Simpsonville, SC, USA @Carolyn Weaver.

It's Time

"There is a season (a time appointed) for everything.... A time to keep silent and a time to speak..." Ecclesiastes 3:1-7 AMP

This is a very personal piece for me – maybe the most personal that I've ever done. The idea came to me as a friend asked me to consider doing a tribute for Corrie Ten Boom, one of my heroes of the faith. As I considered this, an image emerged in my mind's eye, an image of the "Corries" being freed of the "concentration camps".

It is a broken road filled with horrific memories and pain, but as each one walks towards Jesus, He truly brings healing and freedom from the past. It's time for the healing. It's time for our stories of release and freedom to be told, so that many more may come out as well.

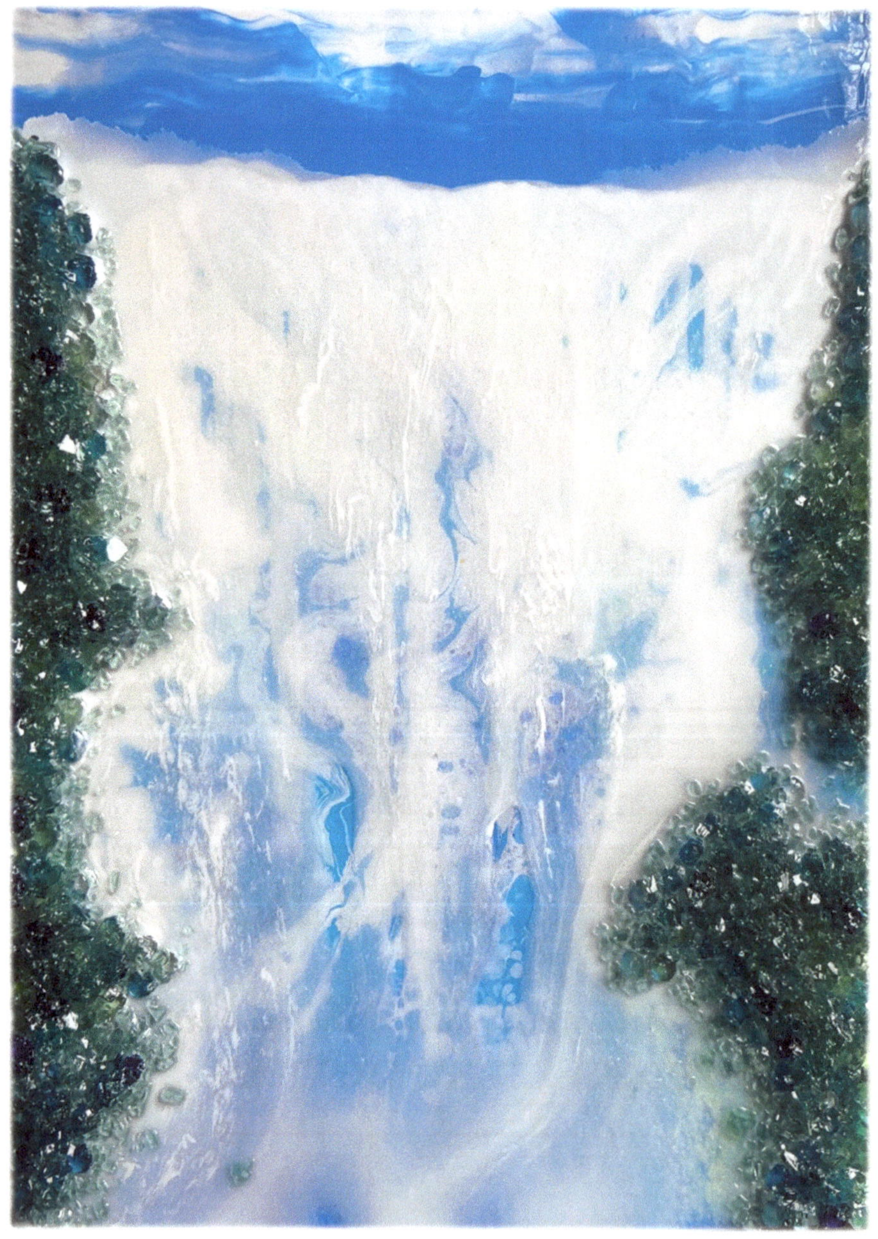

Carolyn Weaver, *The Outpouring*, 2023, Acrylics, 22" x 28", Simpsonville, SC, USA @Carolyn Weaver.

The Outpouring

"And it will be in the last days, says God, that I will pour out my Spirit on all people; then your sons and daughters will prophesy, your young men will see visions, and your old men will dream dreams." Acts 2: 17 CSB

The Great Flood. It's going to happen again, but not like the first flood, not for destruction of the world with water. It's a flood of the Spirit of the Living God like we've never seen.

God sent a rainbow as a promise that He would never flood the earth again in destruction, but the rainbow is also an image of the hope for future promises yet to be fulfilled – the end time flood of His Spirit on all flesh without measure, a flood of His power and justice, a flood of His love and mercy.

Is it beginning to rain?

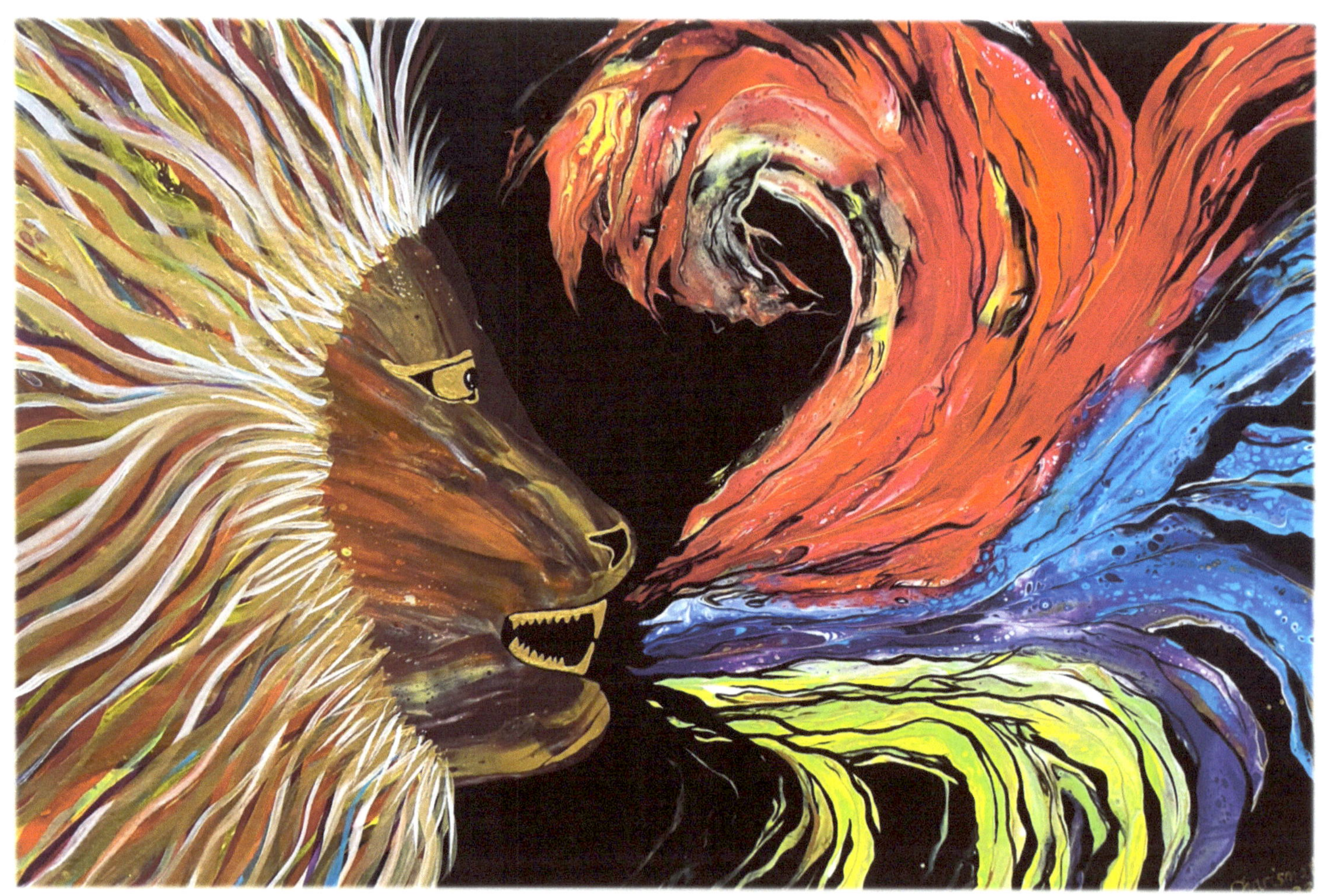

Carolyn Weaver, *The Lion's Roar*, 2023, Acrylics, 23" x 35",

Simpsonville, SC, USA @Carolyn Weaver.

The Lion's Roar

"Then one of the elders said to me, "Do not weep. Look, the Lion from the tribe of Judah, the Root of David, has conquered so that he is able to open the scroll and its seven seals." Revelation 5:5 CSB

"Wrong will be right, when Aslan comes in sight, At the sound of his roar, sorrows will be no more, When he bares his teeth, winter meets its death, And when he shakes his mane, we shall have spring again." (Quote from The Lion, The Witch, and The Wardrobe by CS Lewis, pg. 79)

The Spirit being poured out rolls out the red carpet for the return of our true King!

Truly, the King of Kings, the Lion of the Tribe of Judah is coming. King Jesus is His name. He will make all things right again!

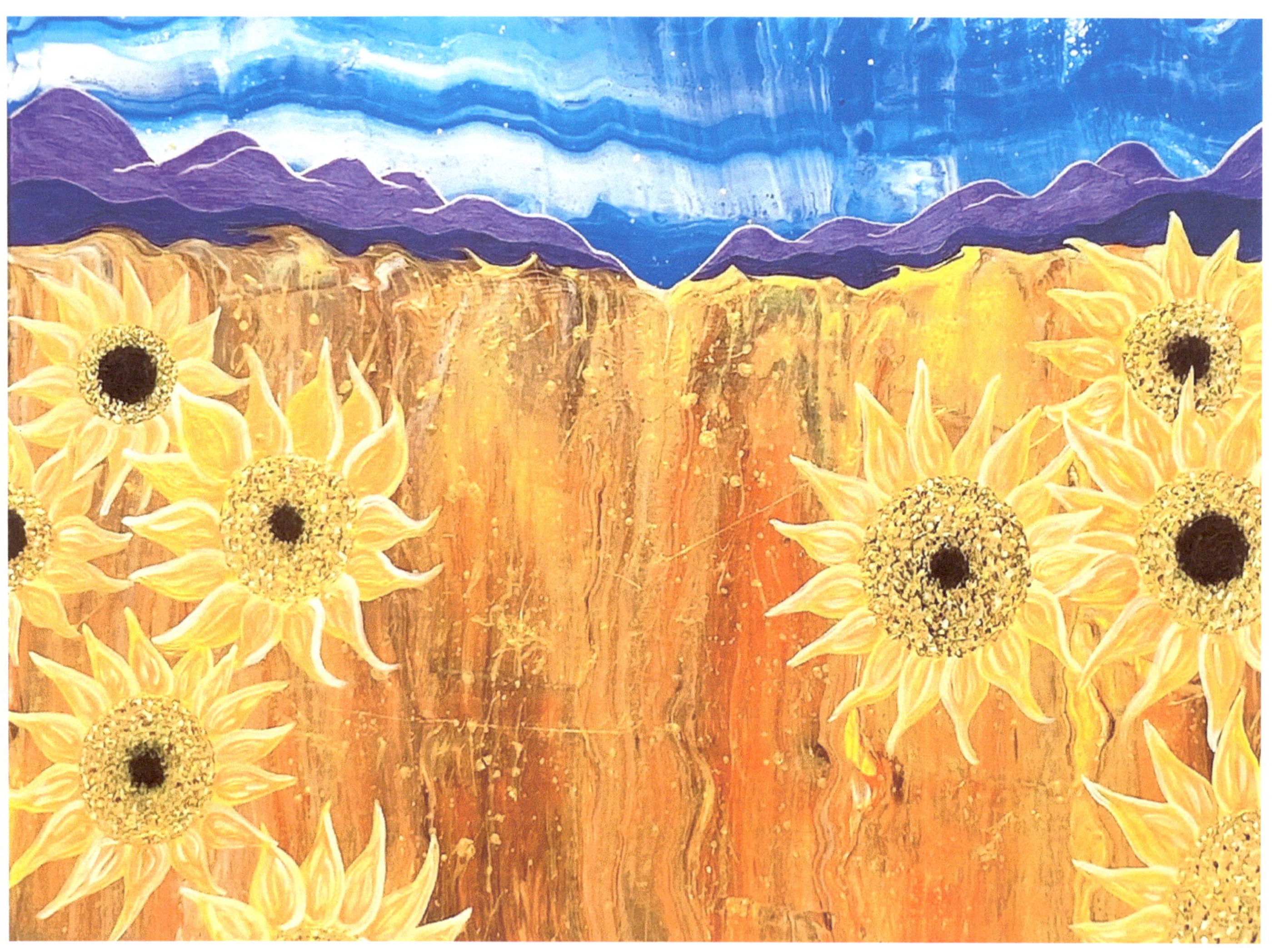

Carolyn Weaver, *The Harvest*, 2023, Acrylics, 30” x 40”,
Simpsonville, SC, USA @Carolyn Weaver.

The Harvest

"The Harvest is plentiful, but the laborers are few. Therefore, pray to the Lord of the harvest to send out laborers into his harvest." Luke 10:2 ESV

Recently, I've been on a difficult path with Jesus, like passing through a deep chasm or valley between two mountains. As we came through to the other side, I asked Him, "Where are we at now?".

"Look!" He said, and I saw myself standing above a great field of golden harvest. Part of that field was sunflowers.

One sunflower can produce from 1,000 to 2,000 seeds, as compared with a wheat plant, which can produce up to 110 seeds per plant. God is saying He's about to multiply the harvest! It will be so very great – none like we have ever seen! Lord, send out your harvesters!

Lorica of Saint Patrick

"I arise today
Through a mighty strength, the invocation of the Trinity,
Through a belief in the Threeness,
Through confession of the Oneness
Of the Creator of creation…

I arise today
Through the strength of heaven;
Light of the sun,
Splendor of fire,
Speed of lightning,
Swiftness of the wind,
Depth of the sea,
Stability of the earth,
Firmness of the rock…"

St. Patrick (ca. 377)

In Conclusion

I hope you've enjoyed engaging with the artwork in this book. I believe all of God's children are designed and able to connect with God in creative ways. He is the divine creator of all, and we are made in His image, with the stamp of creation on us and in us. When we also engage in creating with the Holy Spirit, we have the awesome opportunity to bring heaven to earth, to proclaim His message through the creative expression. In turn, God brings healing to us in ways we didn't know possible.

If you need help in that process, I'd love to invite you to check out my "Encounter" healing art classes on my website, www.blossomingheartsstudio.com. In a safe environment, you can learn to connect with the creator of the universe for yourself and allow Him to set you free.

May you experience God's love in deeper and deeper ways. His love is endless for you!

About the Author

My name is Carolyn Charismata Weaver. I'm an artist, author, and healing art coach.

My passion is to use all the tools God has given me for inner healing with the creative, artistic expression to deepen your connection and experience with the true healer and lover of your soul, Jesus Christ.

I love teaching classes where I lead others into heart healing with God through the creative process.

I've also authored "The Invitation" and "The Bride Arising", which are available on Amazon.com.

To find out more about me, please visit my website at www.blossomingheartsstudio.com.

www.ingramcontent.com/pod-product-compliance
Lightning Source LLC
LaVergne TN
LVHW070202110826
845147LV00002B/473

9781734929751